GW00542315

At the Heart of Montessori

I

Core Principles

by

Clare Healy Walls

ORIGINAL WRITING

© 2008 Clare Healy Walls

Cover image courtesy of Kerry Acheson

All rights reserved. No part of this publication may be reproduced in any form or by any means—graphic, electronic or mechanical, including photocopying, recording, taping or information storage and retrieval systems—without the prior written permission of the author.

ISBN: 978-1-906018-64-1

A CIP catalogue for this book is available from the National Library.

Published by Original Writing Ltd., Dublin, 2008.
Printed by Cahills, Dublin.

*For my grandchildren Seán, Oliver, Turloch, Kalem,
Sarah, Killian, Milla and Ruadh*

CONTENTS

PART 2: THE MONTESSORI PHILOSOPHY

6. Core Principles   31

7. Independence, Freedom and Responsibility   44

8. The Cosmic Plan   55

ACKNOWLEDGEMENTS

Thank you to the many people who inspired me as I learned about the Montessori philosophy over a period of 35 years. I want to pay tribute to the Montessori trainers who taught me the basics, with a special word of appreciation for Mrs. Síghle Fitzgerald, who inspired and still inspires me and many others worldwide, together with Mrs. Connie Fahey who left this world a better place for Montessori students and children. The work of Maria Montessori herself continues to re-inspire me every year but my understanding came through much exploring, day and night, at work and at wonderful parties, with colleagues who have become lifelong friends in Oslo, Gothenburg and Cork. Montessori is a practical science therefore I owe a great deal to the Montessori teachers, trainee teachers and children that I have worked with, in many places, over the years, not least my own loving children who allowed me to learn as they grew. I want to give a special word of thanks to Garrett, Steve and Michal in Original Writing for their creativity, guidance and patience. Lastly thank you to Kerry who portrayed the simple yet profound essence of Montessori's work in her creative book cover image.

ABOUT THE AUTHOR

Clare Healy Walls lives in Ireland. She established Waterpark Montessori teacher training college, which is based in Oslo and has managed this for twenty years. She is a founding member of Montessori Europe. Clare has an MA in Education Management, holds Montessori St. Nicholas teaching diplomas for pre-school and school and has been involved in the development of Montessori programmes for both Infant/Toddler and Adolescent in Scandinavia. Clare holds a special interest in the application of Montessori principles for all age groups, including adults. She is the author of "The Conscious Parent". She has five children and eight grandchildren.

AT THE HEART OF MONTESSORI

I

CORE PRINCIPLES

PREFACE

Dr. Maria Montessori

Dr. Maria Montessori was born in Italy in 1870. She grew up under the influence of a traditional father and an ambitious strong-minded mother. She wanted to be an engineer but found being a woman was an obstacle. However she entered university and qualified as one of the first woman medical doctors in Italy. Her years of study taught her to survive under difficult circumstances. The ethics of the time did not allow for male and female students to work on human bodies at the same time so Maria had to return to the morgue alone at night to do her research. When she qualified she worked for some time caring for the poor in Rome. She was always interested in children, their health and the living conditions which affected health. Around this time she was also involved in the emerging movement for women's rights.

Dr. Montessori had a son but the social structure at the time did not allow her to keep him with her as she was unmarried. He was fostered by a family in the countryside and visited by his mother regularly. Dr. Montessori got a job working with children who were mentally deficient. With her keen observational powers and her ever curious mind, she became interested in their education as well as their health. She studied the works of Itard and Séguin, who in turn were influenced by Rousseau and Froebel. In order to understand these works fully she spent many long nights translating them from French into Italian. She was inspired to research further. She adapted and devised several educational materials which she used with great success with the children under her care. When they passed examinations, Dr. Montessori asked herself why the children in the regular schools could not reach much higher levels with good educational stimulation.

On 6th January 1907 Dr. Montessori opened her first Casa de Bambini (Children's House) in Rome. The owners of a large building were concerned about the small children running wild so they invited Dr. Montessori to carry out an experiment with a day nursery for children in pre-school years. She set up a simple room and into this she placed the educational materials which she had devised or adapted from other educators. She employed the caretaker's daughter to take care of the children and instructed her not to teach them anything, but rather to allow them to use the materials. She observed the children for long periods and added or took away materials according to how the children were attracted to them. The children were shown how to use the materials and, as long as they did not abuse them, were free to use them when they wished.

Within months wonderful things were happening. Children were writing their names, talking about mathematical shapes, behaving very politely and Montessori realised she was making exciting discoveries. People heard about Casa de Bambini and came to see the children. In a world where children were considered noisy and troublesome, these productive well-behaved little people were seen as a miracle. A second nursery was opened by Dr. Montessori the following year. Within a short time she was well known throughout most countries in Europe. In 1911 she published her first of many books, "The Montessori Method". In 1913 she was invited to the USA where she travelled widely, taking her now fifteen year old son, Mario, with her. There she was welcomed enthusiastically and she set up many 'Montessori' classrooms.

In the meantime she started the training of teachers to carry on her method but at all times she was reluctant to allow this training to pass out of her personal control. She believed that her method was not easy to use correctly because it involved a basic shift in attitude towards children. Her observations were continually leading her to adapt and develop new materials. She started to work on the method for older children (6-12 years) as far back as 1912 but believed that it was too big a task for one person. With the help of various interested people, the 'Advanced Montessori Method' was developed over a period of many years. Dr. Montessori was also interested in the next level (12-18 years) but she did not have time in her busy life to explore it fully, writing only two chapters to explain her ideas. However it has been developed since her death, and in the early years of the twenty-first century the Montessori method for adolescents is beginning to grow into a thriving movement.

In the latter part of her life, Dr. Montessori's focus went back to the infant and she further developed her ideas on the first years of life. She published "The Absorbent Mind", the book many consider to be her best, in 1949, just a few years before her death, in 1952. Montessori started in Italy, worked for some years in Spain and spent all of World War II in India. She finally settled in Holland and there, with the help of her son Mario, his wife and many devoted friends, set up a centre for developing the Montessori method.

"Her [Maria Montessori's] ideas were formulated after she had laboriously observed the needs of the individual child. Her goal was to develop the whole personality of the child, and her system is based on her strong belief in the spontaneous working of the human intellect. Her three primary principles are observation, individual liberty, and preparation of the environment." (Hainstock, E., 1986)

Introduction

Clare Healy Walls' infectious enthusiasm for life and keen interest in the welfare of children has encouraged her to share her expertise with others who may be struggling with the noble task of parenthood in the Twenty-first Century.

Clare's accumulated wealth of knowledge in this field comes from her own experience as a parent and grand-parent as well as her ongoing studies as a teacher and lecturer in the philosophy and pedagogy of Dr. Maria Montessori.

In my opinion, Clare is eminently qualified to share her experiences in the field of Montessori education with those who may find the language in text books written in the early Twentieth Century somewhat difficult to understand. Her special style of 'writing as she talks' makes the content of this set of books more attractive to readers. I am happy to recommend these books as a key to a deeper understanding of Montessori's sound philosophy regarding the rearing of children.

Core Principles

Core Principles, the title of the first book in a series of six, and Core Principles in Action, the second book, cover a broad spectrum of Montessori's philosophy of education and its implementation. They envelope the principles of this philosophy, in an attractive and digestible way.

This makes it an easy introduction for the rearing of children and an invaluable reference source for students as well as a refresher for Montessori Educators.

The Infant Toddler Group

Book 3 deals with the characteristics of the child in the period 0-3 years. This is the stage of development when the child is absorbing all that is happening in the environment into the subconscious mind. It covers the period from the pre-natal stage to the third year of life. This is where the foundations are set for all future development.

The Pre-School Child

Book 4 deals with the child of 3-6 years. Montessori considered that the child in this age group should be spending some time at home and some time at pre-school. This pattern ensures an easy transition when the child is achieving a certain degree of independence and freedom essential for the building of the personality.

The Elementary School Child

Book 5 relates to the 6-12 years old child and this is considered to be the prime learning stage. Montessori asks us to look at this period of development in two stages i.e. 6-9 and 9-12 years. This is where the abstract mind is taking over from the absorbent mind of the previous stage. Moral development is the hallmark of this age group.

The Adolescent

Book 6 concerns the quality of the personality and ability of the adolescent which reflects the development that has taken place in the previous years. A strong sense of justice is evident and the great power of the imagination, based on reality, is able to cope with the exigencies of life. Finally, we reach the stage that calls for great sensitivity and kindness in order to build up the dignity of the human person. Montessori advocated a special environment for the adolescent and young adult. She called it 'Erdkinder,' a school of experience in the elements of social life.

"In order to understand the child so as to be able to educate him, we must know life in its entirety" (Montessori, M., unpublished lecture, London 1937)

Montessori looked to the child for guidance in preparing a philosophy of education that would embrace the development of the person from childhood to adolescence.

Síghle P. Fitzgerald, August 2008

AUTHOR'S NOTE

The Hello Montessori series of books is based on lectures I had presented over a period of years. The style is therefore informal and the reader will notice occasional inconsistencies and apparent errors in language structure or punctuation. We ask for the reader's understanding and hope this will not interfere with your enjoyment or learning. An unconventional referencing system is used in many places to facilitate readers in identifying the source of the quotation. There are a large number of editions of the same book by Dr. Montessori, some of them published in the same year and often using varying chapter numbers.

NOTE

At the Heart of Montessori (1 & 2) will help the reader to understand the core Montessori principles and how they are applied generally. In order to understand any of the other four books relating to children of different age groups, At the Heart of Montessori (1 & 2) should be read first.

1. At the Heart of Montessori (1) Core Principles
2. At the Heart of Montessori (2) Core Principles in Action
3. At the Heart of Montessori (3) The Infant Toddler (0-3 years)
4. At the Heart of Montessori (4) The Pre School Child (3-6 years)
5. At the Heart of Montessori (5) The Elementary School Child (6-12 years)
6. At the Heart of Montessori (6) The Adolescent (12+ years)

PART I

MONTESSORI ON HUMAN DEVELOPMENT

I

THE STAGES
OF DEVELOPMENT

1.1. Dr. Montessori and Stages of Development

Dr. Montessori identified stages of development. She believed that these stages were radically different from each other and that children go through a kind of metamorphosis as they pass from one to the next.

Dr. Montessori talks of a re-birth. It is like the caterpillar turning into a butterfly (metamorphosis). It is the same creature after the change, but looks different, acts differently and is a new type of being. The child passes from one stage to another, and at the changeover time, the basic way of being and learning changes fundamentally. The change happens over a period of a few months but the timing is approximately the same for all children worldwide.

The first stage, 0-6 years, is characterised by an absorbent mind and much change. The second stage, 6-12 years, is characterised by a highly creative imagination and a great interest in the social group. It is a stable time. The third stage, 12-18 years, is a time of much change, the emergence of sophisticated rational thinking and huge physical, hormonal and emotional changes. Montessori, in some of the charts she drew, included a further stage 18-24 years in which the young person becomes a fully functioning member of society.

I.2. Table 1a – Diagram of Stages of Development

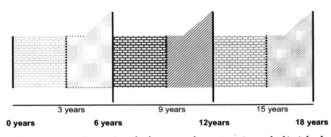

Dr. Montessori noticed that each stage is subdivided. In the first sub-period of each stage (that is 0-3 years, 6-9 years and 12-15 years) the foundations are laid. In the latter part of each stage (that is 3-6 years, 9-12 years and 15-18 years) the child refines what was laid down in the previous three years. (The subdivision at 9 years is not a very noticeable division because children do not change much during the period 6-12 years.) In Table 1a you will see how this pattern of development emerges. Of course children vary and development varies, but this is a general pattern which can be studied to help understand how needs change over the years.

This pattern manifests itself in different motivations and different activities through the stages and their sub-divisions. These are indicated briefly in Table 1b below. This is only a guide and you will encounter some variations in your personal experience. It is useful to study this table and look for these or any other patterns that you can identify from the children you know.

I.3. Table 1b -Characteristics of Stages of Development

First Stage—0–6 years	
0–3 years	3–6 years
Focussing on: ☐ the individual—self-centred	
What is happening? ☐ A time of much growth and change ☐ Health not always stable, vulnerable to infections, illness ☐ Need of emotional protection	
Environment needed: Enclosed	
Main learning tool: The Absorbent Mind	
Basics of social group interaction Basic walking Basic hand-eye co-ordination Basic social interaction Absorbs large amount of information	Refines speech Refines movement Refines co-ordination Refines social graces Refines and orders information

Second Stage—6–12 years	
6–9 years	9–12 years

Focussing on:
- [ ] being a group member

What is happening?
- [ ] A time of steady growth
- [ ] Health stable,
- [ ] Need of emotional protection

Environment needed: The Cosmos / Going Out

Main learning tool: The Imagination

6–9 years	9–12 years
Basics of social group interaction	Refines moral code
Basic of moral code	Refines analysis/abstraction
Basics of analysis/ abstraction	Refines skills of research and learning
Basic skills of research and learning	More focused interest in cosmos
Explosive interest in cosmos	

Third Stage—12–18 years	
12–15 years	15–18 years

Focussing on:
☐ being a member of the universe, of society

What is happening?
☐ A time of much growth and change

☐ Health not always stable

☐ Need of emotional support

Environment needed: Society

Main learning tool: Society

Basics of personal and sexual relationships	Refines personal and sexual relationships
Basic of becoming an adult member of society and finding a role for oneself	Basic of becoming an adult member of society and finding a role for oneself
Basics of higher rational thinking	Refines higher rational thinking

2

BASIC HUMAN TENDENCIES

▓ Basic human tendencies have been identified by anthropologists
and others studying human nature.

Dr. Maria Montessori observed children and noted that they
were attempting to fulfil their human tendencies through work.
At the different stages of development children manifest these
tendencies in different ways. Dr. Montessori noted that it was
important that the correct environment was provided for each
stage in order to allow the tendencies to be fulfilled.

*"The love of activity, the yearning for freedom, the urge
for obedience, the impulse to conform to laws which are
at the heart of all creation – these qualities make man the
unparalleled work of Nature." (Montessori, M., What
You Should Know About Your Child, 1966)*

In this statement from Dr. Montessori you can see how she
believed that the human race had special tendencies, which
made it possible for them to do special things. Much of her
work with children drew out these points, making it apparent
how children could develop these tendencies to their fullest potential and thus improve the lot of the human race.

What are these human tendencies? Dr. Montessori identified eight
areas. Her son, Mario Montessori further developed her work.

2.1. Exploration

This is the human tendency to explore and find out more about the universe and how it works. In the first stage children explore their immediate environment and in the second they want to explore the cosmos by going out or by researching. In the third stage they explore society to find their own role.

2.2. Orientation

This is the human tendency to want to know where we are in space, in time and in the structures of nature and of society. Younger children always want to find that familiar things and people are about them. They like to explore but want to know that mother is nearby. Older children love to find their way in new places, identifying landmarks. They also like to know where they stand with regard to social rules, demanding very clear guidelines and rules. The adolescents need to have a firm orientation regarding limits. They need to know where they stand with regard to adults and peers.

2.3. Order

This is the human tendency to create orderly surroundings which is apparent in nature and which we have brought more thoroughly into our homes and businesses. Children under 6 years of age have a strong sense of order which we can see in all their work. Although the older children are not as tidy as they were when they were younger, they will want to have clear rules. They like orderly work such as mathematics, grammar and classification. Adolescence is a creative time and it is difficult to see order in their bedrooms for example. However, if you watch the habits of dress and the rules of behaviour of an adolescent group, you will find evidence of a strong need for order.

2.4. Work/Activity

This is the human tendency to be active and to seek satisfaction from work. Even rich people who do not need to work will always try to find purposeful activity. One of the most noticeable things about young children in a Montessori pre-school is the manner in which they become so totally absorbed in their work when they find something that appeals to them. Older children become absorbed when the imagination is captured and will spend much energy following through on a project, a football match, or counting the "thousand chain". The adolescents may appear to be lazy at times but when they find work or activity that excites them, they will become enthusiastic and put much energy into this work.

2.5. Repetition

This is the human tendency to repeat things again and again until they become familiar. When a small child becomes absorbed he repeats activities in this way. Have you ever seen a baby deliberately dropping something again and again? Older children can be seen writing pages and pages of addition tables and you have heard a 12 year old playing his first pop record again and again until he knows every word. Adolescents also like to repeat songs many times until they have totally absorbed the emotions in the song. This repetition helps them to get an understanding of the huge emotional changes that are happening to them.

2.6. Exactitude/Precision

This is the human mathematical mind that leads us into exciting scientific discoveries based on precise detailed observation. These are the means by which our civilisation has advanced. The young children are quite precise in the way they pick things up, in the way they describe things and in the way they notice detail. Older children manifest this tendency as they move towards relating abstract ideas to each other, such as they do when they compare multiplication and division. Adolescents become precise when working with science experiments, playing games or handling a baby. They are proud of the how they have refined and developed their bodies and minds.

2.7. Communication

This is the human tendency to communicate not only what is necessary for survival but also as a means of fun and entertainment. Young children focus on communication with intensity, learning the basic tool of language, and also learning to pick up many other signals such as tone and body language. As older children seek to form groups, they use more verbal language with each other than the younger children do. They use it to make rules and establish social relations. Adolescents sway from being very short of words to wanting to speak for hours on one topic. In school, the teachers they love are the teachers who truly communicate at all levels. Communication is an essential human need.

2.8. Imagination

This is the powerful human urge to create new ideas. It is the tool that surges ahead in making humans the 'unparalleled work of Nature'. Young children manifest this by developing the ability to imagine things that are not present and later the ability to imagine things that are merely described to them. Children over 6 years use imagination as the driving force in their learning and will work with enthusiasm on exciting projects about oceans, machines, animals, early humans and so on. Imagination is active in the adolescent although not the primary driving learning force any longer. Adolescents use their imaginations to visualise the complexities of the society they are trying to understand.

3

THE CHILD 0-6 YEARS

3.1. The Infant

> The first six years are the foundation for life. In these six years
> the child develops her basic personality and all the basic skills for
> surviving in the world.

Physically, intellectually, linguistically, emotionally, and socially the child makes huge strides in development in the first six
years of life. The helplessness of the newborn infant is replaced
by a capable young being. The first three years are spent creating the personality and skills, while the next three are given to
refining these. By 6 years the child is ready to move out of the
enclosed environment and into the wider world.

The First Year

Birth and the first hours of life are very important in the
development of personality. We carry memories of our first impressions of life forever in our subconscious. A baby is born
with much effort and sometimes pain. When he reaches the outside world he needs a rest without too many changes. Bright
lights will hurt his eyes, loud noises will frighten him, and cold
hands together with the sudden pull of gravity will add to his

terror. He takes some time to adjust to the world physically and emotionally.

For the first month or more the newborn sleeps a large part of the time and feeds little and often. He moves his arms and legs but cannot turn his body. Sounds are limited to crying or even hiccups. We know that there is much going on inside the absorbent mind, but the infant appears helpless.

From two to six months the baby is awake for most of the day. He becomes quite active physically and reaches out to grasp. The baby now makes cooing sounds, smiles and watches carefully when people talk to him, showing the first signs of socialising. (Dr. Montessori noted that babies in cultures where mothers carry them on their backs all day cry very little.) He will respond to the sound of his mother's or other familiar voices and by six months loves to interact with adults and children.

From six to twelve months the baby learns to sit up alone and then to crawl. Now the world opens up and there are many things to pull, push and bang. He becomes very active in grasping, throwing and banging objects. When he drops something he looks to see where it is gone, showing the beginnings of awareness of cause and effect. During these months babbling is the child's language, when a baby plays with every possible combination of sounds. We often think he is saying "Mama" but it is really only one of many sounds repeated over and over. He understands most simple sentences spoken to him and by one year he is saying a few words intentionally. Socially he is constantly watching, listening and smiling, always anxious for someone to talk to him and play games.

3.2. The Toddler

▌ The Second Year

Physically the child grows stronger during the second year. He moves around all day, crawling, walking, or running. He wants to lift things and co-ordination increases as the child learns to carry out tasks such as feeding himself, putting on clothes, and doing simple puzzles. Intellectually we see how the toddler grows to understand the world and he will spend endless hours experimenting with water or sand, or blocks. A strong sensitive period for order becomes apparent and this indicates that the child is constructing a mental framework for all the knowledge he is taking in. You will notice this sense of order as the child lines up shoes or gets annoyed when you put something in the wrong place.

Language increases rapidly during this year and the child wants to socialise with other children. Lack of language is never a problem in communicating with other children as toddlers use body language very well. However, sometimes there are emotional problems in what has been called temper tantrums. A lack of language, a strong sense of order and a need to become independent often lead to conflict between child and parent. The child needs security and love at this time as he may not understand his own emotions. A child who wants a different plate and is totally unreasonable may not understand that his plate is broken and he does not have the language to communicate his needs. It is also important to realise that this is a year of becoming independent and creating a separate identity. Emotionally it is one of the most difficult years in life.

The Third Year

In the third year the child has become sturdier and moves with agility. Co-ordination is good and the child often starts to dress himself. Intellectually the child develops much greater sophistication, playing imagination games, looking at books and using more complicated puzzles. Language explodes about two years and the child is now, in a sense, an active member of society. He can socialise with people independently of his parents and he is developing his own distinctive personality. Emotionally it is a more stable time than the second year although the child still needs great comfort and security.

3.3. The Pre-School Child 3-6 Years

The child settles down to a period with change, but not as much change as in the previous three years. This is a time for refinement of basic skills and knowledge developed. It is also a time for making right any deviations already created through purposeful work/activity. Physically he grows steadily, even starting his second set of teeth before the end of this period. Intellectually he works with his environment to make conscious what was absorbed unconsciously in the first three years. It is an important time for language as the child increases his vocabulary tenfold and the interest in words and language structure is intense. Emotionally it is a reasonably stable time if a safe enclosed environment is provided with the right stimulation. However, if needs are not being met emotions may spill over into disruptive behaviour. Dr. Montessori called it the period of the 'social embryo' because the social skills were being developed and practised. The children like to play with and exaggerate social customs as you see when they want to play imitation games. They are also laying a basis for social life by developing inner discipline.

▌ Refinement 3-6 years

The child 0-3 years laid down basic skills and the child 3-6 years refines these. This is an important distinction. The child under 2.5 or 3 years is in a completely reality based world. There is quite enough excitement in reality. He does not need refinement as yet.

However the child from 2.5 or 3 years is refining these skills. In movement the focus changes to refining large motor skills, for example hopping, tip-toe, skipping and so on. The child also works very hard to refine his hand movements, especially eye-hand co-ordination. The Montessori classroom has many activities to support this work. Socially the child refines the basic customs absorbed in the first three years. He enjoys the formality of greeting people, saying "excuse-me" and so on. Observe the language of a child from 3-6 years. They have all the basics and now they focus on increasing vocabulary, taking great interest in the precise way a word is pronounced or made up. Based on this Montessori developed her early writing and reading programme.

▌ Sensitive Periods 3-6 years

To correspond with the urge for refinement, the child's principal sensitive periods (periods of intense interest in particular activities) continue right through to 6 years. The sensitive period for movement continues but the focus is now on detail and refinement of movement. The sensitive period for language continues, but the focus is now on vocabulary and how it is constructed. The sensitive period for order also continues, the focus is now an intellectual focus, and the children notice subtle differences such as dark red and light red.

4

THE CHILD 6-12 YEARS

4.1. Characteristics of the Child 6-12 Years

The child of 6 years leaves pre-school in most societies and she enters school. There is a universal recognition of the big changes taking place around 6 years of age. Early childhood is complete.

A metamorphosis, such as happens to a caterpillar when it changes into a butterfly, takes place.

> *"But the changing traits are not so clearly defined in the child as in the insect. It would be more exact to speak rather of 'rebirths' of the child. In effect, we have before us at each new stage a different child."* (Montessori, M., Childhood to Adolescence, 1973)

We as parents, teachers or friends see the babyish child change physically, mentally, emotionally, and socially into a self-sufficient person. Suddenly this new person enters society at a different level.

At the end of this very stable period another dramatic change takes place between 11 and 13 years, continuing until about 18 years. The child enters puberty, a phase of physical, emotional, social, and sexual changes. The period of stability is over.

4.2. Overview of Development 6-12

Physically the 6 year old loses what is commonly termed the 'baby-fat'. She becomes thinner, longer, and stronger. Legs and arms grow especially long. The child's face usually changes, growing thinner and longer.

One of the markers of this phase is the acquisition of a new set of teeth. The milk teeth or first teeth are lost and the child acquires new permanent teeth. The loss of the first tooth is usually an occasion of note for all the family.

Going out, exploring the world metaphorically and actually becomes part of the education of the child between 6 and 12 years. Physically the child is suited to this. She is strong and all her movement has been refined.

▍Cognitive Development

Dr. Montessori discussed the development of the child cognitively in this period, but stressed the emotional, moral, and social motivations behind a child's learning. She believed that cognitive development in this period was powered by the imagination.

> "The mind bases itself on the imagination, which brings things to a higher level, that of abstraction. But the imagination has need of support. It needs to be built, organised." (Montessori, M., Childhood to Adolescence, 1973)

The ability to abstract concepts is a tool of the imagination according to Dr. Montessori, and is central to the Montessori method for this age. However, it is supported by complex systems of classification that help the child to bring order to the vast array of knowledge available.

▌ Social & Moral Development

The social development of the child in the 6-12 years stage is probably the most prominent we can observe. Suddenly from being quite self-centred the child becomes almost obsessed with the group. Friends become of great importance and the rules of the group become the centre of her life. Why does this happen? Socially the child is identifying her role in groups within her society and learning the rules for this. By 6 years the child has finished developing her personality and is now ready to learn about being a member of a group. This is a basic social skill, which will be necessary for adult life.

The moral development of the child in the 6-12 years stage is closely associated with the social development. This is the time when the child starts to differentiate between right and wrong. The limits of right and wrong are obviously strongly influenced by social pressure. Therefore, a time when the child is becoming interested in what her friends think is linked to the development of moral awareness. Not only is the child attracted to join a group, but she is also attracted to the rules and activities created by the group. At this time the human tendency for order tends to focus on the rules of the group. Scouting is one of the activities, which Dr. Montessori believed answered the needs of this age group.

In the 6-12 years phase children are stable emotionally. Unlike the toddler phase and the later adolescent phase, which have many changes, this phase is steady and easier for the children to cope with. Emotions will therefore develop healthily and steadily unless basic needs are seriously deprived.

▌ Language Development

During these years the child needs to:

▌ Develop writing skills such as spelling, punctuation, and structured writing.

▮ Develop a rich language to use for all future learning and communication.

Montessori realised that the child of this age is interested in analysing things so she used grammar as a basis for learning about language skills and enriching the use of language. When we apply the basic principles of inspiration and freedom in learning, language can be a very exciting subject for this age. If there are any problems in reading and writing it is very easy to adapt pre-school attractive materials to help the older children.

4.3. Dr. Montessori and Child Development

6-12 years

Both in child development theories and in structures built up by societies through the ages, one can identify stages of development which approximately corresponds to Dr. Montessori's 6-12 years period.

She was not unique in her observation, but Dr. Montessori highlighted rather special things about the development of the child in this period. As ever she stressed the holistic nature of the development, bringing out three notable characteristics of this period:

▮ 1 The need for wider horizons, to go out and explore the world, the cosmos.

▮ 2 The move from concrete to abstract thinking

▮ 3 The development of a sense of morality closely allied with the intense interest in the social group.

"The three characteristics [...] the child's felt need to escape the closed environment, the passage of his mind to the abstract, and the birth in him of a moral sense – serve as the basis for a scheme of the second period." (Montessori, M., Childhood to Adolescence, 1973)

5

THE ADOLESCENT

5.1. What is Adolescence?

Adolescence is a relatively new concept which has evolved in our modern society of wealth. A couple of hundred years ago children went straight from childhood to adulthood at approximately 13 years of age.

It is no wonder then that some adolescents become rebellious. They have learned many skills to become an adult and yet there are many other skills they do not yet have. Society tends to repress their right to use any of their adult skills up to the day of their eighteenth birthday. However, Montessori and many others have worked to raise awareness of this dilemma.

Montessori believed we needed to look at the nature of the child, in whatever age group he was in, and then give him the freedom and respect he needed. Her philosophy went much deeper than the problems caused by turbulence in adolescence. It is important to realise that her philosophy applies to all age groups. However, she also emphasised that you cannot give respect unless you take into account the natural tendencies and the stage of development of the human being with whom you are dealing.

5.2. The Prepared Environment for the Adolescent

Montessori believed that the adolescent needed two things, "protection during the time of difficult physical transition and an understanding of the society which he is about to enter to play his part as a man" (Montessori, M., *Childhood to Adolescence*, 1973). In helping them to adapt to society she urges that we focus on developing adaptability. We should change the way we look at curriculum. We can make the learning experiences more real so that the adolescent gets practice at adapting to real life situations. Work should be more than intellectual work. She said "All work is noble, the only ignoble thing is to live without working" (Montessori, M., *Childhood to Adolescence*, 1973). She recommended a school for adolescents where they took part in both intellectual *and* manual work, her "Erdkinder" programme which she explains very briefly in her book *From Childhood to Adolescence*. It is a type of farm school that provides a wonderful setting for the best development for adolescents, but unfortunately it is not realistic in most secondary schools in our modern society. However, Montessori schools do try to adapt the principles for their students. A Montessori school for adolescents should provide an opportunity for the young person to experience real life but in a protected environment. This will include outdoor work, intellectual work and opportunities to make a real financial contribution.

The Needs of the Adolescent

Given the fact that the adolescent's body is developing rapidly, this protected environment needs to be a safe and healthy environment. The prepared environment for the adolescent must take account first and foremost of the physical and social / emotional needs. The intellect has reached a new level of reasoning, but intellectual needs have to take a secondary place to the exploding social and personal needs. The intellect should not be neglected; rather it should be stimulated with interesting learning, but not overloaded with large amounts of study.

The huge curriculum imposed on 12-15 years olds in our modern society makes no sense when we take into account the enormous physical and social changes. The children of 6-12 years are better equipped to study large amounts than the adolescents. The adolescent has a new intellectual skill; he is learning the power of reasoning. But that does not prepare him to study large amounts. Instead he needs real life experiences that help him to understand his own role in the society he is about to enter.

If the prepared environment is suited to his needs from 12-15 years, the student will be ready to study the things that really matter from 15-18 years. In reality in our society this is difficult to implement but Montessori schools do try to provide as many real life experiences as possible.

▌ Adolescents and language

The learning of basic first language is normally complete for the adolescent but if not, teachers may return to some of the attractive exercises of the previous stage. At this age a time of great social and personal creativity begins. Language is one of the most useful tools for the adolescent as he explores his creative ability, his own impact on society, and his own inner changes. Language in many forms; spoken, written, drama, and creative language generally, must be encouraged in every aspect of learning for adolescents.

5.3. Comparing the Adolescent to the Infant and Toddler

Dr. Montessori drew some comparisons between the adolescent and the spiritual embryo, the child of 0-3 years. Vital skills are being developed and at the same time there is a deep need for "freedom of movement". Freedom of movement for the adolescent is wider than the exploration of the infant and toddler; however, it has the same elements. In both age groups there is a deep need to explore one's own body, one's own experiences, and one's own reactions. These are internalised and used to create the personality. The infant/toddler is creating his basic individual personality while the adolescent is creating the "social man". Montessori talked about this being a "'sensitive period' when there should develop the most noble characteristics that would prepare a man to be social, that is to say, a sense of justice and a sense of personal dignity" (Montessori, M., *Childhood to Adolescence*, 1973).

The physical embryo and the spiritual (or psychic) embryo have special characteristics. One is an extreme sensitivity to external stimuli. When describing the adolescent, Montessori mentioned "doubts and hesitations, violent emotions, discouragement and an unexpected decrease of intellectual capacity" (Montessori, M., *Childhood to Adolescence*, 1973). It is not lack of intention or desire that makes it difficult for the adolescent to concentrate and study but

> *"[...] a real psychological characteristic of the age. The assimilative and memorising powers of the intellect [of younger children] seem to change [at adolescence]. The chief symptom of adolescence is a state of expectation, a tendency towards creative work and a need for strengthening of self confidence." (Montessori, M., Childhood to Adolescence, 1973)*

5.4. Social and Moral Development

The adolescent is looking for new values and a clear identity and for a time he has no values and no identity. He has abandoned his parental values and has not acquired a new set of values. In this period you may notice the adolescent attaching himself to a set of values with passion. He needs to do this because he feels adrift without values, and catches the first attractive thing that gives a meaning to his floating identity. And hence the pop-star crazes! Opportunities to acquire an identity and a set of values need to be within the experience of the adolescent. It is quite possible for him not to acquire these if not given a nurturing environment with opportunities for real experience. "Adolescence begins at puberty and sometimes ends!" (Gang, P., 1989) There are many people who have never matured beyond the adolescent phase.

Dr. Montessori placed importance on the social development of the adolescent. She also continuously stressed the importance of developing a strong moral character. She refers to 'moral care' which is the "relation between children, the teachers and the environment" (Montessori, M., *Childhood to Adolescence*, 1973). Montessori believed that morality was based on social respect. From this you can conclude that moral care of young people is firstly about providing an atmosphere within which good relations can grow.

Part 2

THE MONTESSORI PHILOSOPHY

6

CORE PRINCIPLES

Montessori's method of education is based on a strong philosophy about the nature of the human being, in particular the child. She had many principles in her philosophy and on those principles her method of education was built. Let us examine the main principles.

6.1. The Absorbent Mind

In her book *The Absorbent Mind*, Dr. Montessori compares the work done by the child in the first six years to that done by university students. She points out that the child does a greater work, and that these first years form the most important part of life.

> *"For, that is the time when man's intelligence itself, his greatest implement, is being formed. But not only his intelligence; the full totality of his psychic powers."* *(Montessori, M., The Absorbent Mind, 1988)*

> *"The child has to construct her own personality and her own "mental muscles". In carrying out this task she uses what she finds in the world about her. We have named this type of mentality, The Absorbent Mind."* *(Montessori, M., The Absorbent Mind, 1988)*

Mental muscles are things like "memory, the power to understand and the ability to think" (Montessori, M., *The Absorbent Mind*, 1988). This amazing type of mind literally absorbs the information of the environment effortlessly, just like a sponge. The child is likened to the photographer while the adult has to laboriously paint or draw his scene.

The child absorbs much information in the first two and a half to three years into the unconscious mind. This is stored in the *mneme*, a preconscious memory. What is stored here is not just put away for future use; it is used to actually create the personality. Adults have experiences and remember them. Children under three years absorb experiences in their very beings.

Between two and three years the child starts to make conscious what was unconscious. The hand has an important part to play in this, and you will notice young children deeply engrossed in something that involves the use of their hands. "The hands are the instruments of man's intelligence" (Montessori, M., *The Absorbent Mind*, 1988)

This sponge-like absorbent mind is the secret of the child's ability to learn so much so fast. The learning takes place from what is around in the environment. The child is driven to seek knowledge and experience from the environment by the *horme*. This is a pre-will energy, which urges the child to move, explore, touch, taste, test and so on. The *horme* is usually much stronger than the need to please adults therefore children repeatedly go back to taste another lump of coal in spite of warnings from an adult. Parents need to understand this drive and not try to contradict it by admonitions and threats. The child is only following her nature.

6.2. The Spiritual Embryo

The Spiritual Embryo (or psychic embryo) is the name Dr. Montessori gave to the evolving personality of the child from birth to three years.

▌ The Physical Embryo

She compared the child in this time to the physical embryo, the first three months in the womb. During these months the physical embryo creates all the basic functions and the basic organs for living in the world. From three months onwards the embryo is called a foetus and develops or refines the basics already created. The physical embryo is in a time of great sensitivity to outside stimuli and certain diseases contracted by the mother in this period, for example rubella, can cause permanent damage to the child.

▌ The Spiritual Embryo

In the same way, the spiritual embryo (the child from birth to three years) creates the basic organs and functions for psychic development. The child is creating the personality. At this time the child is extra sensitive to outside stimuli and can be psychically damaged if she undergoes a severe trauma during this period. Dr. Montessori pointed out the long infancy which human children have compared to other species and explains how this allows the child to co-ordinate the physical and mental sides of their being.

> *"The most important side of human development is the mental side. For man's movements have to be organized according to the guidance and dictation of his mental life." (Montessori, M., The Absorbent Mind, Chapter 7, 1988)*

▌ The Tools to Create a Personality

Dr. Montessori stressed that human children, unlike other species, have to "shape and co-ordinate [their] own movements (Montessori, M., *The Absorbent Mind*, Chapter 7, 1988). The first three years are the time for creation and co-ordination of the personality. The absorbent mind, driven by the horme, is one of the tools, which the spiritual embryo uses for this task. Sensitive periods also play an important role in this process. Another feature influencing the development of the spiritual embryo is *nebulae*.

Nebulae

Dr. Montessori mentions again and again that the child starts out with very little psychic ability, yet creates a personality in a short time. Human children have few pre-determined forms of behaviour but they do have the power to create behaviour. They experience

> *"[...]nebulous urges without form yet charged with potential energy [which] have the duty of directing and incarnating in him, the form of human conduct which he finds in his surroundings. We have called these formless urges, 'nebulae'".* (Montessori, M., The Absorbent Mind, Chapter 7, 1988)

It is in this way that the human child grows to be like her parents, her own community and fits into her surroundings as she grows. The *nebulae* are inherited, but it is left to each individual child to develop these into a personality required for the society in which she is born into.

> *"There is one fact of supreme importance. The nebulae of sensitiveness direct the new-born babe's mental development just as the genes condition the fecundated egg in the formation of the body.* "(Montessori, M., The Absorbent Mind, Chapter 7, 1988)

And that is why Dr. Montessori gave the name "spiritual embryo" (sometimes called "psychic embryo") to the child in the first three years of life.

6.3. Sensitive Periods

▌ What Is A Sensitive Period?

▌ A sensitive period is a time in a child's life when she is especially sensitive to certain stimuli, and is attracted to certain activities.

The *horme* drives the child to selected experiences so that she can acquire certain skills or traits necessary in her development. Hugo de Vries discovered sensitive periods in animals and Dr. Montessori noticed that the child also used these to acquire what was needed to build the personality. This period does not last and is connected to acquiring a particular trait or skill. If the time passes and the child is denied access to whatever her sensitive period is driving her to, she will not acquire the skill.

"It is a transient disposition and limited to the acquisition of a particular trait. Once this trait, or characteristic, has been acquired, the special sensibility disappears." (Montessori, M., The Secret of Childhood, Chapter 7, 1966)

▌ Examples of Sensitive Periods

Children have several sensitive periods. (You may notice other sensitivities to activities later in life but Dr. Montessori used the term for the first six years only.) There are sensitive periods for movement, language, order, cultural mannerisms, and attitudes, noticing small things and others. The best example of a sensitive period is language. A four-month-old baby watches her mother's mouth with intense interest and tries to imitate the sound. From 2 to 6 years she is expanding and refining her language. All this time she is listening to language and attuning herself to the language in her environment. This is how she learns. She is particularly interested in language at this time. Sounds and words fascinate her. If a child is deaf until 6 years it is extremely difficult to learn to speak a language. A child under 6 years of age can learn a foreign language more easily. This is because she is in the sensitive period for language.

█ Adult Awareness of Sensitive Periods

Awareness of sensitive periods will make parents and other adults more understanding of why a child does certain things. A two year old who is angry when she gets the wrong coloured sweater may just be upset because her deep sensitive period for order is offended. Sensitive periods are major learning tools of the young child. They are a special and important time.

6.4. Movement in Education

█ Dr. Montessori emphasised movement as being the basis of all learning especially in the first three years of life.

She stressed that without movement the child was limited in her ability to seek out and receive the necessary sensory stimulation for all development. Lack of freedom of movement also restricts the child's powers of self-expression and interaction with others.

> "Mental work ought to be accompanied by sensations of truth and beauty, which reanimate it, and by movements which bring ideas into play and leave their traces in the external world, where men ought to be giving each other mutual help. " (Montessori, M., The Discovery of the Child, Chapter 6, 1966)

Dr. Montessori also placed great emphasis on the use of the hand in learning. She said all animals could walk, but it was the human ability to use the hand for precise tasks that led to the development of civilisation. She talks about how man's "hands under the guidance of his intellect transform this environment and thus enable him to fulfil his mission in the world" (Montessori, M., *The Secret of Childhood*, Chapter 12, 1966). In her observations of children Dr. Montessori saw that the adult restriction on children's freedom to touch and handle things in the first few years was the cause of so many developmental problems, both intellectual and emotional.

> *"[...] the child's intelligence can develop to a certain level without the help of his hand. But if it develops with his hand, then the level it reaches is higher, and the child's character is stronger."* (Montessori, M., *The Absorbent Mind*, Chapter 14, 1988)

Montessori stressed this point about movement in learning for the younger child but in practice, freedom of movement is basic to the Montessori method at all ages. The involvement of the whole body and, in particular the hand, is essential for learning to take place effectively and efficiently. It is not enough that we provide physical education for part of the day and then confine children to desks while they "learn" intellectual things! The school age child needs movement while learning in order to help concentration to take place, and to help her in co-ordinating the rapidly growing arms and legs. The adolescent needs movement to be part of learning to help her co-ordinate a body that is changing in many ways. She also needs movement to help her focus and concentrate as she struggles to find a new way of relating herself to the world physically, mentally, and socially.

6.5. Normalisation and Deviations

The Natural State for Children

> Dr. Montessori identified that children in their natural state were happy, peaceful and co-operative people with an interest in learning and an ability to concentrate.

She claimed that noisy, boisterous, and fighting children were not the norm. She explained that they had been blocked in their efforts to fulfil the urges of the *horme* and their energies had been deviated.

Deviations of Energy

The toddler who wants to climb and explore but is locked in her cot gets frustrated. The power of the *horme* drives her to do certain things and she is stopped. Therefore, the energy behind the drive gets deviated into other activities. She may become destructive and break things or she may get very quiet and live in a dream world. These are *deviations*. There are many forms of deviation and basically they are all the result of blocked natural energy.

The Process of Normalisation

Dr. Montessori discovered that the child could return to a normal state, which is happy, peaceful, co-operative and able to concentrate. She called this process *normalisation*.

Dr. Montessori did not mean that all children should be the same, rather, that their natural state was something they were entitled to reach. She acknowledged that, given the demands of society, it is impossible for a child to reach 3 years of age without some deviations. However, she discovered that most deviations acquired in those years could be cured in the following three years between 3 and 6 years of age. This process of *normalisation* or "psychic cure" as Dr. Montessori also called it, takes place through work, usually with the hand, and concentration upon an activity. We give the child opportunities to have *purposeful activity* and he will eventually become absorbed in the task and start to *concentrate* deeply. Out of this will come *normalisation*.

"[...] a child's return to his normal, natural state is connected with a single specific factor, that is, his concentration upon some physical activity that puts him in contact with exterior reality." (Montessori, M., The Secret of Childhood, Chapter 23, 1966)

Although normalisation takes place more easily between the ages of 3 and 6 years you will find it is possible to happen at any age. Adults who have completed a successful task that required deep concentration will experience a sense of satisfaction that actually affects the personality. Repeating these experiences can help children, adolescents or adults to find a calm centre in their personalities that allows them to have good self-control.

6.6. Social Development

The Development of an Individual 0- 6 years

Examining Montessori's stages of development will have made you aware of the fact that the child under 6 years is focussing on the development of her own personality.

It is very difficult for children under 6 years to understand the concept of 'sharing', because the *horme* is driving them to take what they need to create their own personalities.

Concentration as a Basis for Social Development

Dr. Montessori believed that the development of the personality was indeed social development. She pointed out that *concentration* was the basis of the social being.

"The first essential for the child's development is concentration. It lays the whole basis for his character and

social behaviour." (Montessori, M., The Absorbent Mind,
Chapter 22, 1988)

When a child learns to concentrate, she gains self-control
and can co-ordinate her own personality. This is the basis from
which she can relate to others in a good way. Dr. Montessori did
not think we should admonish children with phrases like "be
kind to others" because children will do that anyway if their
own basic developmental needs are satisfied. We should concentrate on providing these needs and allow the child to develop
her own personality, including social skills.

Learning Social Behaviour from the Environment

One of the main means of developing social skills is by watching others, therefore, the child is learning from the environment. Parents and minders should take young children to real
life social situations. Bring them to the shop, the workplace, on
the bus, to family parties and so on. A child's greatest learning
happens at these times.

Older children and adults also learn social behaviour from
watching others. But as Dr. Montessori pointed out again and
again, these skills cannot be learned by watching only. Practice
in real situations is also essential.

The Social Embryo 3-6 years

From 3 to 6 years the child starts to rapidly absorb many
more of the skills necessary for the next stage of development.
Dr. Montessori called the child of 3 to 6 years the social embryo. The basic skills and functions necessary for a social life
are being created.

In the first place the child is developing the ability to concentrate and thus develop a co-ordinated personality. The child
also develops an interest in social customs. She wants to know
the right way to do things such as how to set the table, how to
sit, and how to greet people. Montessori schools allow freedom

of choice but with certain limitations. Children may not interfere with others' work, may not damage the environment, and must learn to wait patiently for exercises as there is only one of each item.

> *"[...] the idea of respecting others, and of waiting one's turn, becomes a habitual part of life which always grows more mature. Out of this comes a change, an adaptation, which is nothing if not the birth of social life itself."* (Montessori, M., The Absorbent Mind, Chapter 22, 1988)

The 6-12 year old and social development

The younger child's focus is not on social life. Individual development is more important than social life, but some really important social skills are being acquired. When a child passes 6 years she develops a huge interest in social structures, in particular groups. She wants to be a member of a group, to be part of making the rules and selecting a leader. Dr. Montessori recommended scouting as being particularly useful at this age. Now the child learns how to behave within a group. The rules become interesting in themselves. You often find children of this age playing games like "boys against girls" or "our tree house is better than yours". If they are not cruel to each other, adults should allow these games because they are an important part of learning how to identify with a group.

The 6-12 year old also learns about morality. Morality is based on group norms and rules. The child starts to become very interested in what is right and what is wrong, who is a "goody" and who is a "baddy". In the beginning the view is that all morality is completely black and white. Through the period 6-12 years they start to understand the morality of the culture they live in.

The adolescent and social development

The adolescent is in a special phase where social development is about finding out who she is and especially what her role in society is. She has moved her interest from the small group to the larger society. She explores society to see how she fits in, how the rules affect her and of what importance is she?

Montessori pointed out that the emotional equilibrium that the adolescent is seeking as she grows into an adult, can only come about in situations that allow her to develop naturally and practice her emerging adult social skills. She suggested a farm school that allowed young people to care for animals, work in the outdoors for part of the day, care for others and make some money of their own. All these activities are focused on allowing this young person to develop the social skills she will need in adulthood.

6.7. Language Development

Dr. Montessori spoke about the wonderful process of language development because she believed that language was central to all human development and social life.

"Language lies at the root of that transformation of the environment that we call civilisation." (Montessori, M., The Absorbent Mind, Chapter 10, 1988)

The Sensitive Period for Language

The sensitive period for language lasts for the first six years of life. Regardless of the complexity of a language, a child absorbs her own native language with all its grammatical rules and irregularities, speaking it fluently with a moderate vocabulary by the age of six.

Dr. Montessori's chart of the development of language in the first two and a half years of life in *The Absorbent Mind* explains many stages. To Dr. Montessori, one of the most interesting things was the consistent nature of the development of language in children of all nationalities and intelligence. There must therefore be an inbuilt programme (*nebulae*) for learning language in all human babies that allows children growing up in different countries to learn their own language perfectly.

The child absorbs language intensely in the first two years. During the second year she starts to use many small phrases. At around 2 years most children "explode" into speech and suddenly start to use full grammatical language.

Between 2.5 and 6 years children love words; they are in a sensitive period for vocabulary. They love big words, even when they do not understand them and it is an ideal time to learn to read, if we are careful to make the learning sensorial and suitable to the sensitive period.

When children enter school they should have the basics of reading so they can focus on the many interesting things in the universe that they are longing to explore. Montessori believed that in the years 6-12, children enjoy exploring and playing with language. They love quizzes, grammar games, spelling games, and so on. If children are allowed to explore the world using imagination, and at the same time learn language rules in a fun way, then we find that creative language flows naturally and learning of language rules is easy.

Adolescents are focused on moving into the adult world. They need language as a tool to do that. When they learn a second and third language it will be more meaningful if the learning is related to their other interests. Watch how an adolescent manages language when it comes to the words of pop songs!

At any point in life language is a basic human need. We all want language. How we learn it is based on our needs at the time and the opportunities presented to us.

7

INDEPENDENCE, FREEDOM
AND RESPONSIBILITY

7.1. Independence as an educational goal

Montessori had clear principles on independence, freedom and discipline and self-responsibility. Understanding of these principles is at the centre of making the Montessori method of education work in practice.

The first thing is to understand the philosophy behind these principles. Everything in the method is based on a philosophy and understanding the principles of this philosophy fully is the first part of making the Montessori method work.

What is education? Why do we educate ourselves? Why do we as a society educate children? The answers will vary. Some say education is to provide skills for employment, others to provide skills for life. Another group will say that education is to support the advance of civilisation and yet another that it is to make our lives as happy as possible. You may think it is for all of the above or for another purpose altogether. You could have an interesting debate on the priority of each of these, and if you were to analyse different societies and different modes of education, you will discover that the purpose behind education will strongly influence the manner in which the education is conducted.

Dr. Montessori lived in a society which took part in this debate, but as she observed children, she realised that the goal of education was much simpler than any of those mentioned above. She believed that independence and self-control were the ultimate aims of education; all other aspects of learning will follow automatically if we provide children with these skills. An independent person will seek out education because it is natural to want to learn. Of course we will need to open some doorways to offer access to information, and remove some obstacles to the natural drive to learn. But if we provide the child with the means to become independent, he will educate himself.

"No sooner was the child placed in this world of his own size than he took possession of it. Social life and the formation of character followed automatically [...] Happiness is not the whole aim of education. A man must be independent in his powers and character, able to work and assert his mastery over all that depends on him." (Montessori, M., The Absorbent Mind, Chapter, From Unconscious Creator, 1988)

And indeed the child has an inner drive to become independent so our job is not so difficult. How does the child achieve this independence? Through activity! It is an ongoing process throughout life. The core of independence is laid in the first six years but we must continuously allow activities that develop more and more independence. Dr. Montessori points out that nature demands freedom and independence, it being a law of life.

"How does he achieve this independence? He does it by means of a continuous activity [...] Independence is not a static condition, it is a continuous conquest." (Montessori, M., The Absorbent Mind, Chapter, The Child's Conquest of Independence, 1988)

7.2. Freedom according to Dr. Montessori

Once you have fully accepted, with your whole personality, that the child will educate himself if he is allowed to develop independence, you will have become a true *Montessorian*. But that takes many years. However, in the meantime try to accept this fact with your intellect! If the principal goal of education is to become independent and if the child has a natural urge to become independent, the way to educate is to allow the child to follow his natural urge. That means we must offer the child freedom. In fact Dr. Montessori links independence and freedom.

What kind of freedom do we offer the child? There must be some limit to freedom. However, limits to freedom do not mean that we cut down on the freedom in a negative way, rather we offer limits as a positive means of feedback. The freedom itself must be complete. One of the most important quotations from Dr. Montessori explains this:

> *"When we say the child's freedom must be complete, that his independence and normal functioning must be guaranteed by society, we are not using the language of vague idealism. These are truths revealed by positive observations made upon life and nature. Only through freedom and environmental experience is it practically possible for human development to occur."* (Montessori, M., The Absorbent Mind, Chapter, The Child's Conquest of Independence, 1988)

This is a difficult concept to comprehend but with patience and practice the Montessori teacher eventually gains a deep understanding of the nature of freedom. Dr. Montessori believed it was very difficult for adults to understand the real nature of freedom as we have been so far removed from nature. The main task for us as educators is to keep our own goals clear, being aware of our in-built prejudices and fears.

"[...] we must not project into the world of children the same ideas of independence and freedom that we hold to be ideal in the world of adults [...] Their idea of freedom is a very sorry one. They lack the breadth of nature's infinite horizons. Only in the child do we see reflected the majesty of nature which, in giving freedom and independence, gives life itself[...] She [nature] makes of freedom a law of life; be free or you die!" (Montessori, M., The Absorbent Mind, Chapter, The Child's Conquest of Independence, 1988)

Dr. Montessori wrote these words about the child under 6 years. However, although the basic character has been laid, the child of 6-12 years, or even the adolescent, is closer to nature than the adult and will therefore be able to accept freedom more easily than we can. We must, as teachers, be aware that the older child may have already built up fears of freedom. The adult society has been projecting these fears onto the child. Therefore when we offer freedom to the older children or adolescents, it may take some days or probably weeks for them to start to use it properly. We, the teachers, can help in this period by offering the right kind of limits, but *not* by reducing the freedom.

7.3. Discipline balancing freedom

Too often Montessori teachers interpret limits to freedom as negative rules. Limits to freedom should be presented in a way that makes them a point of interest rather than a restriction. Managing freedom is learned by getting feedback from consequences or the limits of the world. Dr. Montessori believed that error was such a natural part of life and such a wonderful learning mechanism that she deliberately built a 'control of error' into her materials. The control of error has another side benefit. It becomes a point of interest in itself. It encourages concentration. And as Dr. Montessori pointed out the children will soon understand that errors in teachers and in children are quite natural. We learn from them.

Dr. Montessori spoke strongly against rewards and punishments. She believed that they were superfluous. She said prizes insulted the free child. He may ask for approval, but prizes and unasked for praise distract from the true goal; the joy of the work in itself. Punishments and grading of work were to Dr. Montessori not only useless, but quite harmful.

Self-discipline is the ability to control one's own will. With practice, just as in any other skill, the will develops. Yet the child cannot practice the use of the will without activities and the freedom to choose them. We cannot improve a child's will by lecturing or even by good example. A strong character and self-discipline are built by having opportunities to practice freely chosen activities in a structured environment, and the freedom to learn from one's own mistakes and not depend on others for praise or punishment.

7.4. Learning self-responsibility

When children are given freedom and are allowed to develop independence they will firstly learn self-discipline. Out of this will grow self-responsibility. Independence is essential to develop self-responsibility. Responsibility is about the ability to 'respond' to a situation with an appropriate action. It means that one does not avoid the response by passing the problem on to another or by just ignoring it. Responsibility is a trait of a strong character. It depends on a well developed will and a lack of fear about 'being blamed'. To develop a sense of responsibility for oneself the child must in the first place be independent. Then he must be free to make choices thus developing his will through practice. When the child had developed independence and strong will, he is ready to take responsibility for himself. The next hurdle is the level of responsibility that the adult will allow him to take.

We all probably agree that a sense of responsibility is important for children to eventually become 'good citizens'. The key question for most adults is when to give the children responsibility. If we are willing to observe the child, and if we are willing to give up our own control, we will find that the child tells us when he is ready to take responsibility. It is part of the 'continuous activity' working towards independence.

Another issue is deciding what the responsibility of the child is and what the responsibility of the adult is. The child's behaviour is the responsibility of the child. The adult's behaviour is the responsibility of the adult. The adult is responsible to offer good example, to create limits, to enforce limits when necessary, and to allow the child to act freely. Then the adult has done all she can. Now the child is responsible to behave within that structure. Dr. Tony Humphreys explains this:

> *"It is not the teacher's job to control children ... closer examination of the traditional discipline practice reveals that it is a recipe for conflict to get one person to control another [...] Effective classroom management is based on the principle that each member of the class, student and teacher, is responsible for his or her own self-control."* (Humphreys, T., 1993)

We hear teachers saying "I am responsible for 25 children". What she means is "I am responsible for setting up conditions for 25 children to learn, and responding to the needs of these 25 children to the best of my ability." This slight shift in thinking will help you as a teacher to give the children a sense of responsibility. This is difficult for the adult to understand at first. However if you do understand it you will find it easier to offer the child the freedom and respect which is his right. It is worth spending time analysing many of the children's activities which we 'take responsibility' for.

We must be ready to stand back when we see the first hints of a child wanting to take responsibility. We must stop ourselves from wishing to protect the child. Adults often judge that a child is 'too young', ignoring the wishes of the child. Remember that our judgment is based on society values and is not as wise as nature. If we observe the child and listen to our own true instincts we will make the right judgment. We should not listen to the voice of fear imposed by society, for example "What will my friends think of me letting a child of 8 years travel alone?"

There will be occasions when the child wishes to take some responsibility, but wishes the adult to be nearby. We, as adults should be there to offer security, but try not to substitute our personalities and take over.

> *"An adult can substitute himself for a child by acting in his place, but also by subtly imposing his own will, substituting it for that of the child." (Montessori, M., The Secret of Childhood, Chapter, The Substitution of the Personality, 1966)*

7.5. Building self-esteem

▌ Lack of high self-esteem has been established as one of the main causes of problems in modern society.

> *"[...] the well-being of all human systems is determined by the level of self-esteem of each of the participants of a particular system." (Humphreys, T., 1993)*

High self-esteem is undermined by lack of freedom to become independent, criticism and fear. Dr. Montessori explains how the adult interfering can undermine a child's confidence. Adults often see children as weak and wish to impose their ways upon the child. Adults fail to offer the same respect and courtesy to children that they do to other adults. Therefore the child, at a very sensitive period of his life when his personality is being formed, absorbs the impression that he is worth less than others.

*"A child [...] must notice with a continued sense of frus-
tration that he is the only one thought to be unreliable
and a source of harm [...] feels that he is different from
the rest of mankind, that he is inferior, subject to all."*
(Montessori, M., The Secret of Childhood, Chapter –
Deviations, 1966)

Be aware also of the fear imposed by society on the child.
Dr. Montessori stresses the dangers of fear. She points out that
a direct threat can be responded to by the child. But our ways of
imposing fear are usually more subtle. We undermine the child's
confidence with unanswerable subtle threats.

*"[...] these children cannot escape the feeling that they
are intellectually inadequate [...] if you don't do these
exercises well, if you don't study these lessons properly,
I won't put you in for the exam' – it is impossible to
answer such an argument. It is not a threat, it is a conse-
quence. This state of mind grows more and more pervasive and causes insecurity."* (Montessori, M., The Child,
Society and the World, Chapter, On the Schooling of
Young People, 1989)

Fear undermines confidence leading to misbehaviour, delin-
quency, bad relationships and dependency. It is the worst enemy
of independence and good self-esteem. Yet it is an integral part
of the way our society works. Fear within us as adults is hard to
recognize and to remove. It is one of the main reasons we need
to work on our own personal development in order to become
true Montessori teachers. We must become aware of how our
fears influence our attitude to the child and of how the older
child's own fear is creating an obstacle on the road to independence and responsibility.

*"In our state schools, we cultivate fear, and this is not an
insignificant factor but a real danger. For if someone has
a tired mind, he has an inferiority complex, he is afraid*

of the superior human being, he is afraid of not knowing how to <u>respond</u>." (Montessori, M., The Child, Society and the World, Chapter, On the Schooling of Young People, 1989)

The level of self-esteem is crucial to the functioning of people within society. We can encourage self-esteem by encouraging independence and through offering freedom and respect. We have noted that Dr. Montessori sees the basic respect due to a child as being essential in building strong character. Dr. Tony Humphreys would support her view although he puts it in a different way. He stresses that teachers must, at all times, avoid behaviours that put down self-esteem such as scolding, ridiculing, taunting, labelling, ignoring, and so on. He also suggests that all our dealings with children ought to give encouraging messages such as:

- You belong
- You are capable and you please me
- You are unique and special
- You have a right to your own unique way of developing
(Humphreys, T., 1993)

You will note that the stress for building self-esteem is not on praise. Rather it is on respect for the child, allowing him the right to develop independence in his own way. Praise puts the dependence on the teacher's point of view. The teacher may tell the child, if asked, "I like your work, I believe it is very interesting. What do you think?" This is a personal statement rather than a judgment. Dr. Montessori recommends that the teacher, when asked for approval should

"[...] respond with a word of approval, encouraging him with a smile, like that of a mother to her baby. For perfection and confidence must develop in the child from inner sources with which the teacher has nothing to

do." *(Montessori, M., The Absorbent Mind, Chapter, Discipline and the Teacher, 1988)*

The child needs to learn that he is capable and lovable whether the teacher thinks so or not. The child must eventually rely upon his own opinion of himself, not on the opinion of adults.

7.6. Independence in social and moral development

When studying the moral characteristics of the child 6-12 years, you discover that he is learning a framework of moral values based on the needs of others. This is a natural development and with it come a need and a right to make one's own decisions.

> *"In the second period [6-12 years] there exist, then, possibilities superior to those we used to know in the child. Only, these possibilities are subordinate not to the command of someone, but rather to the command of the child's own conscience." (Montessori, M., Childhood to Adolescence, Chapter, Moral Characteristic, 1973)*

We can trust the child; he has a conscience and an intelligence of his own. Let us stand back and allow independence and responsibility to grow.

On the other side of the medal we can see that this conscience will be impeded in its development if the child is not free to make his own choices. When a child is subject to the demands of another's will, the conscience gets no practice and will not develop fully.

Independence is an integral part of social development. Dr. Montessori wrote about the spontaneous formation of the group amongst children 6-12 years. This is the centre of learning of social skills for the age group. However, it is an essential part of the process that the child freely chooses to be a part of the group. If he does not choose freely, he will not be willing to accept the rules of the group and it will become another exercise done to please or obey adults. And he cannot choose to belong to the group if he is not independent and free.

Likewise the belonging to the social group will enhance the child's independence. The activities which the group wishes to carry out involve going out, making plans and rules without adults, and creating mini social structures. The younger children learn skills of independence from the older children; the older children practise and refine these skills with the whole group.

8

THE COSMIC PLAN

8.1. What is the Cosmic Plan?

Dr. Montessori had a deep philosophy that underlies one of the main principles used in Montessori schools over 6 years, cosmic education.

The cosmic plan is the name given to the plan, which governs everything in the entire cosmos. There are different beliefs about what designs or governs that plan ranging from God through to 'Mother nature' or 'pure chance'. Dr. Montessori was quite specific in her views. She never advocated one religion over another, but she believed firmly that there was a divine power or plan behind everything in the cosmos.

"But here we have another factor – not visible but immaterial. This is the Spirit, The Divine Spirit, intelligence, acting, guiding. The tiniest creatures have their guide which leads them on step by step." (Montessori M., The Child, Society and the World, 1989)

The cosmic plan includes everything from the nature of the developing child, to the rising of the sun each day, and to the strange behaviour of plants in the Amazon. Above all it is about the manner in which all things in the cosmos are connected, connected to each other and connected to the plan.

8.2. Dr. Montessori and the Cosmic Plan

▌ Dr. Montessori wondered ceaselessly at the incredible intelligence behind this cosmic plan, its beauty and its order.

Her theories on the child and the inbuilt mechanisms for development are closely connected to the existence of such mechanisms throughout the cosmos. Her main controversial theory around the cosmic plan was about the place of 'man' (humankind) in this plan. She believed that the special intelligence given to humans had an enormous impact on the evolution of the earth. She saw this as a positive impact of which humans were sometimes unaware. She points out that cosmic theory gives recognition to humanity for all its efforts, while religion attributes everything to the mercy of God. She said that humans were involved in the creation of this 'one organised energy', but seemed to fret about their useless efforts.

> "[...] instead of being a parasite, he is the one who not only enjoys the environment, but is the most active of the agents who are destined to modify and perfect it [...] one thing still evades the intelligence of humanity and that is the consciousness of their terrestrial destiny and of the fact that the whole of humanity is so intimately united that it forms but one organised energy. The revolutionary movements of our days are a sign of the great crisis from which 'the Universal Consciousness' of humanity is about to be born." (Montessori M., The Child, Society and the World, 1989)

Dr. Montessori said this in 1946. Many years later there is strong evidence that her vision was absolutely right. Human consciousness is indeed expanding rapidly towards this universality. And amongst other things, the internet is one of the tools that humans invented that created a leap in this development.

8.3. Interdependence of All Things – Formation of a Unity

▌ An essential element of the cosmic plan is the interdependence
of all things.

Humankind is one organised energy bur it is wider than that. All cosmic matter, all cosmic energy and all cosmic events are part of one organised energy. In fact energy, matter and events are all one. Quantum physics, one of the major breakthroughs in physical science of the twentieth century, shows us that what we thought was solid matter is in fact a bundle of vibrating energy particles. These particles are so minute that we cannot distinguish whether they are matter or energy. This is further evidence of the unity of all things. We have all heard about the theory of relativity which tells us that time is only relative. What a contradiction to earlier beliefs that time passed inevitably. Now we know that it is dependent on space and movement.

"The 'new' science has developed the capability of confirming the pervasive unity which embodies the universe – as foretold by our religious and mystical ancestors. Relativity theory and quantum physics provide us with a new window to view the interdependencies. It tells us, at one and the same time, that we know more about existence than we have ever known and that existence remains, and may always remain a mystery. Matter and energy become interchangeable, as particles and waves of energy are sometimes indistinguishable." (Gang, P., 1989)

So, the cosmic plan is about unity of physical existence, of all living things, of humanity, of everything in the cosmos. In fact Dr. Montessori, more especially towards the end of her life, having worked for many years observing children, believed that this philosophy was the solution to world peace and harmony. Human society, when examined in a historic perspective, shows that it has been evolving towards this unity all through the ages.

8.4. Order in the Cosmic Plan

Order is a basic human tendency according to Dr. Montessori. Indeed few would argue with her on this. Order is evident in everything in the universe. There is order in the solar system, in nature, in the young child, and in the systems we have put in place in our civilisation.

Where there is chaos, order tends to move in and regain control. It would seem that the cosmos uses chaos in an orderly way. Chaos creates opportunities for new formations, new ideas and creativity. The order principle in the cosmos then brings it back to a format in which life can continue in peace.

We can relate this principle to the earth after a big fire in a forest. We can relate it to the child listening to many stories and eventually deciding on a theme for her study. We can relate it to our personal lives when we go through a chaotic time but then we settle down, having gained some creative ideas from our chaotic period. We must learn to trust order. It will always come back because it is an inherently basic principle of the universe and of all life. We can afford to allow some chaos into our lives as we learn to trust order. To Montessori this trust in order was basic to creating the optimum environment for children to grow in true dignity.

8.5. Cosmic Balance –Finalistic and Causalistic Forces

Finalistic force: This is nature's force, unconscious, internal. It is about putting things together to reach a specific end.We can see a finalistic force as being predestined to a specific end. It is an expression of creation. It is in each of us by nature when we are born. It is the source of our personality and physical construction. (Pestalozzi, the Swiss educator of the last century, first used this phrase in connection with children at work).

Causalistic force: This is the external, conscious environmental force. It is about the relationship between cause and effect, as experienced by us in the environment.

Basically these two forces are directions of energy. We may talk about a baby constructing her personality. Two forces are working, the inner drive (finalistic) and the outer experience of the environment (causalistic).

In nature we can see that both forces play an important role. When birds migrate at the end of the summer, which force drives them to do so? When a bird's nest is invaded what force is at work? But then when the parents abandon the eggs, what force makes them do so?

Dr. Montessori spoke in Perugia in 1950, shortly before she died, about the need to reconcile these two forces. Her focus was on the inner energies, the finalistic force, but she stressed the importance of the environment as this is the impetus or "push" (the causalistic force) that urges the child to put the other force into action.

The Montessori teaching method attempts to use both forces, but emphasises that the drive comes from the finalistic force. Many 'traditional' teaching methods focus on the causalistic approach. Examine which force is in play when a child is cleaning a window, having a group discussion, doing her checkerboard for mathematics or doing a project. What force is being used when the teacher tells an inspiring story about Early Man (Humankind)? Or when the teacher is demonstrating the Pink Tower to the child?

8.6. Ecology and the Cosmic Plan

▎ Ecology is about the balance in nature created by all living things
interacting with each other, helping each other to survive.

There is a natural balance created in which there is just
enough of life's essentials, such as food, water, oxygen, space,
warmth, and so on for the species within a particular ecological
unit or system. Units may be as small as a tiny pool or as large
as the entire universe. The same principles always apply.

Problems arise in ecological balance when one species is
withdrawn from the unit or an outside force interferes with the
balance. There is much concern nowadays about the human in-
terference in the balance of nature, particularly when introduc-
ing foreign substances. Chemicals belong to the universe, but
they are contained in certain places and in quantities that are
balanced in an ecological sense. On occasion humans upset that
balance when they dump large quantities of one substance in a
place where it cannot be absorbed naturally

The cosmic plan is all about balance and unity of energy. It
creates an overall plan that incorporates the needs of all things.
Of course there are adjustments all the time and it may seem
that there is an imbalance. But the balance will be restored.

Dr. Montessori believed that humans were coming to a stage
of consciousness where they would understand their contribution to the balance of the cosmos. She identified human intelligence as being the unique contribution of our species. If used
correctly and with a sense of pride in this special role, such intelligence would be a natural part of the evolution of the cosmos.

In his book *Rethinking Education*, Dr. Philip Gang develops
the idea of four ages of humanity relating to nature. They are:

- The age of humanity <u>in</u> nature (First humans – hunters
  – gatherers)

- The age of humanity <u>with</u> nature (First farmers – Early Civilisations)
- The age of humanity <u>over</u> nature (Industrial Age)
- The age of humanity <u>through</u> nature (New Age of Consciousness/ Age of Information)

Dr. Gang points to the Information Age as being a part of the bridge to this new age of consciousness. This approach also shows a positive attitude to the human contribution to the cosmos.

"It is an era in which humanity has an opportunity to understand its role in the evolution of this planet. That is, we can begin to awaken to our personal responsibility to protect the earth from further deterioration. It is a time of a knowing participation in nature, a realization of nature through human nature." (Gang, P., 1989)

8.7. What Is Cosmic Education?

Froebel first coined the term 'cosmic education' when he wanted to describe the unity of our knowledge and its inter-related nature. Cosmic education is what Dr. Montessori devised as a method to present the cosmic plan to children and to use it as the chief means of their education in the period 6-12 years. In the first place she believed that an understanding of the cosmic plan was essential to all people and in the second place that the child aged 6-12 is ideally suited to this kind of learning. She also used cosmic education as a basis for her plan for educating adolescents but in a slightly different way. She even suggested we use a cosmic approach within a sensorial framework for the preschool children. To Montessori a cosmic approach was the most natural and basic approach to all education.

9

IMAGINATION, FANTASY, CULTURE
AND CREATIVITY

9.1. What is the Imagination?

"We often forget that imagination is a force for the discovery of truth. The mind is not a passive thing, but a devouring flame, never in repose, always in action." (Montessori, M., The Absorbent Mind, Chapter, Through Culture and the Imagination, 1988)

> Imagination is a power of the mind. It is the power that allows humans to go beyond the confines of their physical form and to be part of a wider world. It is the power that leads humans to create new ideas and new ways of living.

Dr. Montessori believed that it was important to understand that the imagination was an integral part of the human mind and of the human personality. She strongly disapproved of those who would separate the imagination from intelligence. She said that in that way we restricted what the imagination could do and we removed an inspiring power from the intelligence. Nowadays, even though we have made advances in our holistic way of thinking about education, there is still a tendency amongst some adults to see imagination as belonging to the so-called 'creative' subjects, art, music, drama. These same people tend to see mathematics, grammar, physics and other 'logical' subjects as being nothing to do with imagination. Imagination acts as powerfully when doing a geometric theorem as when painting a picture.

> *"The secret of good teaching is to regard the child's intelligence as a fertile field in which seeds may be sown, to grow under the heat of flaming imagination." (Montessori, M., To Educate the Human Potential, Chapter, The Right Use of the Imagination, 1973)*

9.2. Fantasy and Imagination

Imagination as a Human Power

Imagination is a powerful force, which drives the learning of the older child and it is also used by the younger child under six years to create mental pictures of a world she cannot see. Imagination is a special human power, which needs to be fed with plenty of real life experiences so that it can develop. When we use the word fantasy, we mean situations and people and things that do not, and usually could not, exist. If a child is exposed to too much fantasy, the food for her imagination is fantasy and she can get trapped in the limited cycle of another's creation.

Reality versus Fantasy

Dr. Montessori believed that we should give the child reality to fire her imagination. The child should make a real meal rather than playing with a doll's tea set. The child who gets stories of a farmer sowing his wheat or of dinosaurs who roamed the earth is excited and encouraged to use her imagination to expand on these stories. We do not need to tell her stories based on make-believe creatures because this will confuse her. In adult life we are exposed to some fantasy, but most of our life is firmly grounded in reality. Young children are attracted to reality and will learn to enjoy it and use their own imaginations to create new situations in their own lives without having to live excitement through fantasy creatures.

Fantasy for the Younger Child

Another reason for limiting fantasy for children under 4 or 5 years is that they very often cannot tell the difference between reality and fantasy. We may tell them a story of an imaginary creature and they may believe it is real and be afraid of it. The adult is not always aware of this because he has forgotten how limited the child's experience and powers of judgment are. Whilst a seven year old may be fascinated by a story of a huge 'creature' at the door, a three year old is fascinated by the story of a man at the door. Central to Dr. Montessori's theory on fantasy is the belief that we do not need to offer fantasy to a three year old – life is exciting enough anyway. Dr. Montessori believed that many adults offer fantasy to children in order to satisfy their own needs. Children believe them because they do not know any better just yet, they are what Dr. Montessori called 'credulous', which means they will believe anything they are told because they know no better! In this case the adult is taking advantage of their innocence.

Dr. Montessori did not want us to abandon all our traditional fairy tales and nursery rhymes. She simply said we should be careful. Why offer too much fantasy when reality is more attractive and better supports other development?

"The creative imagination cannot work in vacuo. The mind that works by itself, independently of truth, works in a void." (Standing, EM, 1962)

9.3. Imagination as a Learning Tool

The absorbent mind is the chief learning tool of the child 0-6 years. It is the means by which learning is facilitated. Likewise the imagination is the chief learning tool of the child 6-12 years. Learning is in fact facilitated by imagination throughout life. But in the period 6-12 years, the logical reasoning powers have not developed therefore the imagination dominates the learning arena.

> *"Imagination is the great power of this age. Since we are unable to present everything, it is up to the child to use his imagination. The instruction of children from seven to twelve years of age must appeal to the imagination."* (Montessori, M., Childhood to Adolescence, Chapter, The Passage to Abstraction, 1973)

The adolescent is also inspired by imagination. Although there is a sudden increase in logical reasoning power at 11 or 12 years, the adolescent up to 15 or 16 years is quite confused and has not yet put this reasoning power into a manageable structure. Therefore imagination still plays a dominant part in learning for adolescents.

We should never forget that imagination plays an important part in all learning and creative thinking throughout our lives. Einstein, in spite of his high intelligence level, could not have made the "quantum leap" which led to his discoveries without imagination.

9.4. Imagination and Abstraction

Imagination is the power that makes it possible for humans to abstract concepts from practical realities. Humans are conscious beings and imagination is one of the tools of that consciousness. Dr. Montessori stresses that the imagination needs a structure to work within and her plan for cosmic education includes these elements. She states clearly that imagination is the power that brings humankind to great levels but that this cannot happen without organisation.

> *"The mind bases itself on the imagination, which brings things to a higher level, that of abstraction. But the imagination has need of support. It needs to be built, organised. Only then may man attain a new level. He is penetrating the infinite."* (Montessori, M., *Childhood to Adolescence*, Chapter, *The Passage to Abstraction*, 1973)

We start with the whole and then move to details in cosmic education. These details provide a framework within which the child can hold a clear view of the whole. Classification and other "precise keys for study" are the structures within which the imagination will thrive (Montessori, M., *Childhood to Adolescence*, Chapter, The Passage to Abstraction, 1973). The imagination, working from a base of precision and order, is able to take in the world of reality and abstract from it concepts and ideas. The imagination is a power that can mix perceptions and ideas to create new concepts. Then out of the details the imagination will take us back to a new "whole", a new inspiring big story.

9.5. Imagination and Creativity

Imagination is a power that leads to creativity. Ideas are abstracted and than converted into reality again. This is creativity. Take for example a child who sees a picture of a woolly mammoth and hears a story of cave dwellers and how they hunted the mammoth. She also has a dog at home that she loves and she knows from her personal experience that animals like being with people. She imagines and abstracts ideas about the possibilities of woolly mammoths interacting with people based on a mixture of what she has learned. She is learning language skills and now uses them to write a story about a woolly mammoth as a pet for a cave family. Not only does this story satisfy her need for creativity, but it provides a stimulus for further creativity and further research into the Old Stone Age.

The creative mind should not be seen as the opposite to the logical mind, rather it is a partner. Imagination is the power behind these two parts of the mind. Intelligence might be seen as the overall container.

9.6. Fantasy or Reality

Dr. Montessori had a reputation for being opposed to fantasy. She used the word fantasy as being unreal thoughts, thoughts on things that did not happen. She did not anywhere object to the child creating objects of fantasy but she objected to the adult feeding the child somebody else's fantasy instead of feeding her exciting reality. She also had a problem with adults presenting fantasy to children without making it clear that it was fantasy. Children under 5 years confuse reality and fantasy. For the older child Dr. Montessori did not object to fantasy, but she wanted us to limit the fantasy in proportion to the level of fantasy in real life. There is so much exciting reality out there, why present all that fantasy? Fantasy in literature has much value to older children and adolescents, but not to the exclusion of the wide range of exciting facts in the universe.

Imagination is a power, which should be honoured and given exciting reality based food. Dr. Montessori believed that imagination not based on reality wanders aimlessly in circles and cannot focus.

> *"A mind that is habituated to seek pleasure only in fantastic tales, slowly but surely becomes lazy, incapable of nobler preoccupations." (Montessori, M., To Educate the Human Potential, Chapter -The Right Use of the Imagination, 1973)*

9.7. What Basis for Reality?

Dr. Montessori was quite specific in what she suggested as the means for keeping contact with reality, and ensuring that that reality was not boring.

She said that practical life activities are the basis of everyone's life and should be presented to the younger child as exciting exercises. (Practical Life activities are activities that help the child to learn to carry out everyday tasks in his life). For the older child (6-12 years) she wanted us to continue practical activities and this included activities around 'going out'. 'Going out' is an important part of school activity for children 6-12 years. When a child is learning to check her sleeping bag, her food and her compass as she prepares to go on an outing, she is working on the structures within which the imagination can thrive. If her food were forgotten, her imagination would be suffocated by hunger pangs! But if the practical details are taken care of, the outing can be a source of elevating inspiration and creativity.

"Going out" preparation exercises as above are at a more advanced stage for the adolescent. They know how to prepare for outings but it continues to be useful in helping them to contain their energy and to focus their minds. In addition Dr. Montessori recommended that the entire school for adolescents (*Erdkinder*) should be based on a practical life solution. Adolescents are to be involved in running a guest house, a shop, a farm and any other suitable small enterprise. The advantages of these activities are many. But in this context they provide a practical way of focusing imagination in a reality base.

Sensorial exercises provide what Dr. Montessori called an 'alphabet of impressions' for the real world. In the same way that practical life activities provide the outer physical structure for imagination, sensorial exercises provide the mental structure. Sensorial activities are designed for 3-6 year olds, but are useful for children as terms of reference up to 7 or 8 years. The older child (6-12 years) will revisit sensorial materials through mathematics and once again be provided with inspiration in a concrete form. Later the adolescent will use these materials in an exploratory imaginative way, seeking practical concrete solutions to problems. Once again we are providing a reality base for the imagination.

Cultural subjects is a term used in Montessori circles to incorporate all cultural aspects of the child's education, but it tends to be used to refer specifically to science, art, music, history and geography. These subjects form an essential part of the Montessori curriculum of inspiration. Sometimes in a Montessori school for adolescents these subjects tend to become "subjects" rather than sources of inspiration. This is partly because there is a large curriculum to cover and partly because there are different teachers for different subjects. Montessori teachers can try to solve this problem by using a cosmic integrated approach to teaching and by allowing students to guide their own work whenever possible.

9.8. Culture as Part of Social Life

▌ By culture we mean all the ways, mannerisms and tastes of people.

Culture is about the way people do things. It does not have to be about great art or music. If parents love Mozart then Mozart is part of the child's culture. But if RAP music is what her parents like, then that is part of her culture. But of equal importance is the way to use a knife and fork, the way to greet people, the way to behave in public. Every nation has its own customs and ways of doing things. Likewise every district and social class will have small variations. We see this most obviously in the language used or accents from different regions. But observation will quickly tell you that there are cultural differences in almost everything people do. And for a young child this is of particular relevance because this is the time when she is learning her own culture, its language, customs and tastes.

For the younger child culture is to be found in the immediate environment. For the child under 3 years this will be her home and the local places she is taken to. For the child of 3-6 years this will expand a little to include playmates and preschool. She will also start to absorb the social norms in her culture. For the child of 6-12 years culture is everything in the universe, but with particular emphasis on the things that relate to her and her life. For the adolescent, culture is about social customs that provide a place for her. She will seek out the music of her own day because it helps her to relate to others of her age, giving her an identity within society.

10

INTELLECTUAL DEVELOPMENT

10.1. What Is Intellectual Development?

What do we mean by the intellect? Do we measure intelligence by the level of development of the intellect? Is intellectual development the same as cognitive development? When we speak of the intellect do we mean the 'thinking' part of a human being?

Cognitive development is more commonly used nowadays when referring to our ability to think. Noirin Hayes defines cognitive development as "a process involving perception, memory and concept formation" (Hayes, N., 2005). We will use the term 'intellectual development' because Dr. Montessori used that term. However, 'cognitive' and 'intellectual' are interchangeable in this context.

Donald Hebb developed ideas around the different aspects of intelligence not unlike those of Dr. Montessori.

"For Hebb, Intelligence A represents an innate potential which depends entirely on neurological facilities and signifies a capacity of an individual to develop intelligent responses [...] Intelligence B represents a hypothetical level of development which has resulted from the interaction of Intelligence A and environmental influences." (Child, D., 1981)

There are many books written about intellectual development so we will confine ourselves in this chapter to Dr. Montessori's views. Modern thinking on intellectual development is quite close to Dr. Montessori's views, but remember that she always saw any development in terms of the whole human being. Modern research has also developed many in-depth approaches to certain aspects of the intellect. Technology has made great progress since Dr. Montessori's day, and this too has made important contributions to modern research. Recent discoveries about brain development in infants have developed Dr. Montessori's ideas in more depth, but her thoughts are still absolutely valid.

Of course there are innumerable questions about whether it is possible to separate the intellect from other functions or not. Montessori stressed that it was not possible to isolate the intellectual functions from physical and emotional functions. But for the purpose of studying intellectual development we need to be able to discuss the intellect in its own right. We will always assume that intellectual development is interdependent with other aspects of development. Holistic development is central to Montessori education – and Dr. Montessori developed what might be argued as one of the best approaches to holistic development.

> *"[...] the mind is unity, a whole, not divisible into a number of separate mental faculties, such as Memory, Reason, Attention and Association of Ideas, each to be consciously trained."* (Montessori M., To Educate the Human Potential, Chapter, The New Psychology, 1973)

10.2. Order and Intellectual Development

Jean Piaget spoke about the mental processes that we use to build up our concepts. We *assimilate* information (that is we take it in) and then we *accommodate* it (that is we adjust what we have learned previously in order to fit in this new information). (Hayes, N., 2005) As new information comes in we will find the accommodation process easier if we have our previous information in an orderly arrangement.

Dr. Montessori stressed the need for order in intellectual development. She said the sensitive period for order is necessary for the child to learn new information and to gain control of the world he lives in. The child demands order and consistency and therefore is better able to take in new information at a pace that he can handle.

> "A sensitiveness to the orderly arrangement of things, to their relative positions, is contemporaneous with simple perception, i.e., with the first taking in of impressions from the environment." (Montessori, M., The Absorbent Mind, Chapter, Through Culture and the Imagination, 1988)

You can picture your mind as somewhat like your desk drawer where you keep many papers. You may have some very useful information you got from a friend in a letter. If the drawer is so untidy that you cannot find the letter, the information is not available to you. It is the same as if you had never got it. Or else it takes so long to find, that you think it is not worth it. Then one day you tidy your drawer and now you can find what you have, and you can find it quickly. Your intellect works a little bit like that, it is, of course, more complex and sometimes our intuitive brains make leaps that do not seem related to order at all. But overall, order is essential to humans for the construction of the intellect, especially when there is a great deal of new information coming in.

The human mind is mathematical by nature. It is orderly and needs order for its proper function. It is also creative but the creativity needs the mathematical aspect of the mind to get it out into the world. It is for the development of this mathematical mind that the *materialised abstractions* (Dr. Montessori's description of her own sensorial and other materials) were designed.

10.3. Making Conscious what was Unconscious Knowledge

In the first three years of life we absorb huge quantities of information into our unconscious minds. All through life we continue to store some things in our unconscious minds. We need to make some of this information conscious or it cannot be used by us in our daily lives.

Making conscious what was unconscious is one of the tasks of human life. Carl Jung declared that if we do this throughout our lives, it will be a more satisfactory life that we live. He claims it is a natural process of the special type of consciousness that humans have (Storr, A, 1998).

Children spend much of their time bringing unconscious knowledge to consciousness. All learning involves some of this process. We usually reflect new information within our unconscious. The process of learning brings out whatever was reflected in the unconscious. But the time when this happens on a large scale is between 3 and 6 years. The process actually starts before 3 years and continues throughout life, but this three-year period is where we can observe it happening all the time.

There is so much information stored in the unconscious in the first three years, the child needs to bring much of it to consciousness. The main way this happens is through activity, most commonly activity with the hands. The child who is building a tower of bricks becomes aware of the fact that the smallest brick on the bottom makes the tower fall. He may have been building that tower for some time and it may have been falling. But now he consciously thinks "I must put the big one first". Dr. Montessori says:

> *"It is as if the child, having absorbed the world by an unconscious kind of intelligence, now 'lays his hand' to it." (Montessori, M., The Absorbent Mind, Chapter, From Unconscious Creator, 1973)*

10.4. Dr. Montessori and the Psychology of the Unconscious

Dr. Montessori did not claim to have discovered a new psychology of the unconscious, but she explains what she calls 'modern psychology' (as was in 1948!) in her own words, showing how such principles have been incorporated into her schools since her method was first initiated in 1906. She describes three 'mental factors'.

▓ The Mneme

The first factor is the *mneme*. This is the unconscious memory that stores everything that happens to the individual.

> *"All the experiences through which an individual passes in life are retained in the mneme, not only the infinitesimal part that enters the consciousness. "* *(Montessori M., To Educate the Human Potential, Chapter, The New Psychology, 1973)*

She points out that things which we learn may not stay in our memory, but we do retain a certain power that makes us quick at learning things related to these 'lost memories'. So the experiences we have remain as traces in the *mneme*, and these traces give the mind the power to function well. These traces are called *engrams*. So it is these *engrams* that make the intellect grow, giving it a power rather than just an accumulation of facts.

Dr. Montessori then points out that the child in the Montessori school, who is repeating many activities relating to the same topic (for example several ways of doing addition), will have a series of related *engrams* in her unconscious mind.

▌ Élan Vitale

The second mental factor is *élan vitale*. Dr. Montessori takes this term from the philosopher Bergson. *Élan vitale* is a vital urge, which every living creature has. It is not a direct will but is a stronger sub-conscious urge. It drives the living creature, human beings in our case, to seek experiences to create *engrams*. It is also known as the *horme*. Dr. Montessori uses the term *horme* to describe the pre-conscious will, which the child has in the first two years of life. When Dr. Montessori discusses *élan vitale* she is talking about all humans, not just little children. *Élan vitale* comes into play when a person is urged to go back to university and study at forty years of age. *Élan vitale* is active when a child is urged to use different materials in a Montessori classroom. That is why the exercises must be attractive, well presented and why the child must have the freedom to spontaneously choose her work.

▌ Association of Ideas

The concept of *association of ideas* resembles Piaget's ideas on association but is more specific. Dr. Montessori says that psychologists think (in 1948) that *engrams* are more important to the process of thinking. *Engrams* associate spontaneously when the mind becomes interested in something. In the association a new route is created and a new idea is created. This process has been explored in much more depth by modern brain research but essentially the process is the same.

You have probably experienced in your own life that if you left a problem alone for a while, the solution just 'came to you'. By leaving the problem you allowed the *engrams* to go on working in the unconscious. They had provided the solution when you returned to the problem. The most creative thinking happens in this way.

Using the example of the child learning how to do addition, we can see that *engrams* have been created in the unconscious. No single *engram* tells the child that 7+8=15, but traces of this have been left. Then the *engrams* spontaneously associate one day when the child is particularly interested in addition. All the experiences of 7+8=15 come together and the conscious mind can access the result. Now the child 'knows' that 7+8=15.

It is worth stressing here the importance of spontaneous choice and of a variety of attractive purposeful activities to allow this process to work naturally. The teacher does not teach, rather he allows the process to happen. It is on points like this that we must see the deep importance of the principles of practice that are implemented in the Montessori classroom.

10.5. Abstract Ideas from Concrete Materials

Dr. Montessori designed a wide range of beautiful materials for sensorial education, mathematics, language, biology, history, geography and anything else that was possible to teach by creating a *materialised abstraction.*

All the materials have the same purpose, to help the child to develop himself. They are not simply aids to the teacher in presenting knowledge to the child. They are designed to represent a mental concept in a material three dimensional form. The materials are designed to encourage independence and self-directed learning and have a particular purpose. You can make Montessori materials in your own home but you must have a thorough understanding of Montessori's principles behind materials before you can do this successfully. The materials must have certain very special characteristics.

The child under 6 years is in a sensorial concrete learning phase of life. The child of 6-12 years is in a phase of using the imagination to form abstract concepts. The adolescent is moving into a phase of abstract reasoning. But all throughout childhood, in fact all throughout life, our minds are abstracting ideas from concrete materials. You do it every day of your life as you go to work, brush your teeth or read a book. Our minds are active instruments that want to know how and why. By forming abstract concepts and ideas, we can make frameworks into which the many things that happen in the world can be fitted.

However, children form abstract ideas in different ways at different stages. Up to the age of 3 the child needs the concrete object available to be able to hold onto the concept. It is difficult for a child of 1 or 2 years of age to understand that all swans are birds, but all birds are not swans. A name for something is the child's way of keeping the idea conscious and when the label becomes abstract the child is confused.

From 3-6 years, some common or generic abstract ideas are being formed. The child that matches red colour tablets is making the concept of 'red' conscious. He has been meeting red things since birth, but now he is made conscious of the fact that red is in fact a quality. Language helps to hold onto these new conscious concepts, which is why the three-period-lesson is so important at this age. (The three-period-lesson is a Montessori technique for teaching vocabulary.)

The child of 6-9 years is making a big leap into abstract thinking. However, you will note that although a child may be able to abstract the concept of what a verb is, he will find it much easier to remember if he has coloured symbols to help him 'ground' the abstract idea.

By the time the child is in the 9-12 years stage, he is able to form abstract ideas with some ease. In this phase the child sees the concrete images and forms an idea abstracted from these. This abstract idea usually stays in the child's mind without the ongoing support of the concrete image. However, when the concept is a difficult one to grasp the child will need the concrete support for some time. Therefore, something as complex as the structure of a molecule, will need a diagram to aid the child's understanding. Later he will form a mental image and will not need the diagram.

Then as the child passes 12 years and moves towards adulthood, he develops the power of deductive reasoning. Some adults never reach this stage. Deductive reasoning involves many layers of 'what if' reasoning and in this case there may be no concrete image to support the abstraction of ideas. Such reasoning develops well after the age of 12, if it is built on the firm foundation of abstracting ideas from concrete images.

10.6. Classification of Impressions

▚ Sensorial Education

Sensorial education is a basic part of Montessori's method of education. In all her books Dr. Montessori stressed the importance of sensorial education. It is not just about refining senses, it is also about intellectual development. Sensorial materials are a beautiful collection of materials that present isolated concepts about the world to children in a way that allows them to explore and experiment until they have fully taken in the concept and made it conscious. These materials are designed around the experiences of the five senses and the concepts we have built around these sensorial experiences. Colour tablets help the child to understand the "redness of red", to understand the quality of red.

The child of three has collected many facts. They have been collected in as orderly a way as the child could manage. The sensitive period for order is quite strong, but given the fact that the mind absorbs everything, there are many facts in the mind, which are not in any order. Dr. Montessori points out

"Now, abstract ideas are always limited in number, while the real things we encounter are innumerable." (Montessori, M., The Absorbent Mind, Chapter, Through Culture and the Imagination, 1988)

The child has an unlimited number of impressions in his mind. He needs order on these or they become confusing. Sensorial education sets out to limit the number of ideas by making the child conscious of qualities. A child knows the ball is big, red, and soft. That helps to categorise that ball amongst all the other objects in the environment. The same applies to verbs, words and ideas. They are defined in some way and the number of things to be held in the mind is reduced. This is closely associated with the whole process of making conscious what was unconscious. To know a ball consciously it needs to be defined in some way.

▌ Classification

This need for intellectual order was felt so strongly by Dr. Montessori that she built it into many other activities in her method of education. To her classification was an ideal means of keeping mental order, holding onto large amounts of knowledge, and it also became a most useful point of interest in Montessori exercises.

The human tendency for order is in each of us. We need and want order. How else could we cope with this vast world? We have an in-built mathematical mind which demands that we think in an orderly way.

Children in the preschool classify. Sensorial education is about comparing and discriminating. These are the functions the child uses in pairing, grouping, and grading. So the child is not confined to the traditional sensorial materials, but can group cards of domestic and wild animals and vegetables that grow over the ground and under the ground. Then they learn parts of animals and plants, discovering which animals have feathers, which have scales and so on.

When children pass 6 years and move into the phase where they expand widely intellectually, classification becomes even more important. Grammar is a classification exercise whereby children sort words. Not only does it help them to understand grammar better, but it is fun and creates an interest in words and their functions. The creating of the orderly system grounds the knowledge and makes a structure from which creativity can grow.

Biology is the subject where classification becomes the most useful. Scientists decided a long time ago that they needed classification in order to manage the vast array of animals and plants in this world. Children from an early age do exercises to group animals and plants. This grouping becomes more complex. They have to think about the characteristics of the animals or plants in order to decide to which category they belong. At the end of the 6-12 period the children do exercises that bring together all their knowledge in the 'Tree of Life'.

Adolescents should work with classification exercises to help them to sort their vast knowledge. The advanced classification exercises from 9-12 classes are very useful for the adolescent pupils. In addition to this the exploring reasoning minds of the adolescents will be interested in the whole idea of intellectual order and the creating of concepts. This means that you can present an adolescent with a piece of sensorial equipment (for example a colour box with pairs of colour tablets) and explore with them how it helps to develop the intellect. In fact many adolescents would enjoy discussing intellectual development. They love to explore themselves and how they function.

These exercises are important, not simply for the wonderful knowledge they give the child on biology, grammar and so on, but for the mental structures they create. *Engrams* have been formed and will remain in the unconscious. Even when the child has forgotten about the animals, the potential to categorise things by their characteristics is still there. This, surely, is a key to intelligence.

10.7. Supporting Intellectual Development in Practice

Ideas on intellectual development are based on Dr. Montessori's and others' views on how the intellect is formed.

However we must come back to the practical aspect of this theory. The role of the Montessori teacher is to put these principles into practice. The role of the adult is often one of holding back rather than being an active teacher. This also applies to supporting intellectual development.

It is more important to develop the skills of thinking rather than passing on knowledge. When the child has developed the skills of thinking he will be able to get his own knowledge. And he will be able to do this more easily than if we were 'teaching' him. If we accept this, we will need to give energy to supporting the kind of intellectual development that Dr. Montessori describes. The exercises we give to children should be designed to create *engrams* rather than to impart information. Of course the exercises can both create *engrams* and be informative but we must not measure success by the amount of knowledge learned.

The next step for the teacher is to focus on the exercises and materials. They must be attractive and should encourage repetition. The teacher must present them in a clear, decisive and inspiring manner. In fact you should give more attention to the materials than to teaching the child. That is how you will serve the child's intellectual development. If the child is attracted to these experiences again and again, the *engrams* will be formed. The intellect will develop to its full capacity.

Finally, if this whole process is to work, it must be a natural process, based largely on unconscious processes that cannot be controlled. Making the conditions right can encourage these processes. Then the child's natural in-built mechanisms for learning must be allowed to work. This means that you must allow spontaneous activity. If you choose the work for the child, his *engrams* cannot associate spontaneously because his interest is not strong enough. Freedom of choice is essential. A spontaneous choice made by a child is one that will produce the best results. The job of the adult is to create an atmosphere where that can happen.

II

KNOWING THE CORE PRINCIPLES

▌ Dr. Maria Montessori had a wide ranging philosophy on human development and in particular on child development.

She developed many special theories on how the child functions and it is these principles that need to be examined to understand the Montessori philosophy and method of education. She built her work on a few basic principles discovered by observing human life and its natural tendencies for many years. These are principles of life and of education. She consistently stressed the importance of the practical application of these principles. She believed that children under-develop both personally and intellectually because we do not follow the principles that nature provided for development.

Having examined the different stages of development through infancy, childhood and adolescence, it is possible to see that Montessori had her own particular approach, emphasising certain patterns that she saw in human development. The stages of development give us, the adults, a framework within which we can understand children. These stages are not exactly the same for all children but they help us to identify general needs.

The human tendencies are very broad human traits that will help understanding of how humans work. It is useful for all those working with children, teachers or parents, to take a look at human nature and then to try to understand how children function within that framework.

It is not easy to understand all Montessori's principles in the beginning. Some of them require a new way of thinking. They make common sense but are rarely common practice in our society! In the next book of the Hello Montessori series, *At the Heart of Montessori – Core Principles in Action,* we move on to look at how the principles are put into action with children. As you read and as you reflect upon what you read, you will find that you will understand the principles better. The connection between theory and practice is especially relevant for Montessori education as it is a method based on *"materialised abstractions".* The theory and the principles help us to make the method work in practice, while the practice and observation of children help us to understand the principles more fully.

BIBLIOGRAPHY

Child, Dennis   Psychology and the Teacher
                         Holt, Rinehart and Winston
                         London   1981

Gang, Philip S.   Rethinking Education
                         Dagaz Press, Vermont   1989
                         ISBN 0-9623783-0-5
                         Out of print-
                         e-copy available- <ties@ties-edu.org>

Hayes, N.   Early Childhood, An Introductory Text
                         Gill and Macmillan, Dublin   2005
                         ISBN 0-7171-3932-8

Hainstock, Elizabeth   Essential Montessori
                         Plume Printing, (Penguin)   1986

Humphreys, T.   A Different Kind of Teacher
                         Carraig Press, Cork   1993
                         0-7171-2489-4

Montessori, M.   What You Should Know About Your
                         Child
                         Kalakshetra Publications, Madras   1966

Montessori, M.	The Secret of Childhood	
	Ballantine Books, New York	1966
Montessori, M.	The Discovery of the Child	
	Kalakshetra Publications, Madras	1966
Montessori, M.	From Childhood to Adolescence	
	Schocken Books, New York	1973
Montessori, M.	To Educate the Human Potential	
	Kalakshetra Publications, Madras	1973
Montessori, M.	The Absorbent Mind	
	Kalakshetra Publications, Madras	1988
Montessori, M.	The Child, Society and the World	
	Clio Press, Oxford	1989
	ISBN 0-7171-2835-0	
Standing, E.M.	Maria Montessori, Her Life and Work	
	New American Library, New York	1962
Storr, Anthony	The Essential Jung, Selected Writings	
	Fontana Press, London	1998